Piece of Pie à la Mode

More Layer Cake Friendly Quilt Patterns

Brenda Bailey & Bonnie Bailey

Pie Plate Patterns

Piece of Pie à la Mode

More Layer Cake Friendly Quilt Patterns

Copyright Brenda Bailey and Bonnie Bailey 2009
All rights reserved.
Published in the United States of America by Pie Plate Patterns, Fountain Green, Utah

No part of this book may be reproduced in any form without written permission from the author(s), whether or not you profit from it. The written instructions, photographs, designs, patterns and any other illustrations are intended for the personal use of the retail purchaser only and are protected by U.S. copyright laws.

Printed by Peczuh Printing, Price, Utah

ISBN: 978-0-9820835-1-2

Pie Plate Patterns
PO Box 31
Fountain Green, UT 84632
info@pieplatepatterns.com

www.pieplatepatterns.com

We have made every effort to ensure the accuracy of the instructions in this book. Please notify us of any inadvertent errors in the instructions so we can correct them.

We welcome your comments and suggestions and would love to see pictures of your finished projects.

Introduction	4
Heart 2 Heart	6
Dash Away	10
Arizona Trail	14
Peas in a Pod	18
Boston Commons	22
Wall Flowers	26
Final Four	30
Slice & Dice	34
Simple Simon	38
Yours Truly	42

Table of Contents

> "The desire to create is one of the deepest yearnings of the human soul. No matter our talents, education, backgrounds, or abilities, we each have an inherent wish to create something that did not exist before."
> —Dieter F. Uchtdorf

A year ago, we attended a meeting where we were challenged to become the best at *something*. The speaker told stories about people who had taken this challenge to heart and had accomplished extraordinary things. He gave us only two rules: 1 - make your decision carefully and with a lot of prayer because once your decision is made on what you want to be the best at, you can't change your mind. 2 - video games and texting are not options.

We were inspired by this challenge and made up our minds quickly. Though we aren't the best at quilt designing, we are following the rules and sticking to our decision; we hope that we are facilitating the success of others by igniting creativity within themselves. Maybe, just maybe, we can help you in some small way to become the best at *your something*.

When we published our first book, Piece of Pie: Layer Cake Friendly Quilts, in 2008, we had no idea if anyone would even be interested in our Layer Cake designs. Fortunately, it has been very well received, and we have been able to put 10 more projects together for those of you, like us, who are having a *blast* making quilts using Layer Cakes. Use the innate creativity you've been given to make these designs your own.

We are showing our true colors with the name of our company: *Pie* Plate Patterns, and the products that we have been using to design our quilts: Layer *Cakes*. It seems only fitting to include even more delicious dessert recipes with these new designs. ENJOY!

All quilts pictured are made with: Warm & White Needled Cotton Batting provided by The Warm Company.
www.warmcompany.com

A Special Thanks To:
Andrea Law
Shannon Simmons
Denis Andelin from Mansion House Photography
Our family for random things we make them endure such as: being a quilt rack for a picture, stepping carefully over the quilt that is laid out on the living room floor, assistance in choosing border fabric, writing bios for us that make us chuckle, etc., etc., etc.

*Photographer's Note:
All of the "candid" shots of our quilts were taken in our little town of Fountain Green, Utah. The front cover picture is taken in our yard. Our sheep camps have been home to many.

Layer Cakes

*A Layer Cake is a bundle of 40 - 10" squares of fabric.

*A Layer Cake is equivalent to about 3 yards of fabric.

*Layer Cakes are perfect for those of you who love the "scrappy" quilt look.

*If you struggle with selecting fabrics for your quilting projects, then using a Layer Cake is a perfect solution. Since the fabrics are all from the same line, they will be easy to work with, will wear the same and will look great together.

*You can make your own Layer Cake from your fabric stash. Just cut 40 - 10" squares. They don't all have to be different fabrics. There are Layer Cakes that have some duplicates as well. You can also buy 1/3 yard of 10 fabrics and cut 4 - 10" squares from each piece.

*Some of the patterns in this book use all 40 Layer Cake squares, but some don't. For these quilts, pick out the squares you like to provide the finished look you want. Example: If you are using a light background, you may not want to use the lighter Layer Cake squares in your quilt.

Pay attention to the Layer Cake pincushions for helpful tips.

*Since Layer Cake squares have pinked edges, we suggest that you measure your Layer Cake squares using your own cutting tools. This way you will know exactly where the 10" measurement is - on the points or on the v's of the pinked edges. Taking time to measure before you begin cutting will help you avoid a lot of headaches later on.

*Often, you will have background pieces the same size as your cut Layer Cake pieces. If they aren't exactly the same size, use the background pieces as your guide as they are usually more accurate.

*One of the most difficult things about using Layer Cake squares in your quilt is laying out the blocks when they are finished. Often, the same color or the same fabric design will end up next to each other. So, take your time in laying out your blocks and move them around until you are satisfied.

*If the pattern uses less than 40 Layer Cake squares, you can make extra blocks with the remaining squares. This will give you more options when laying out your blocks. You can use the left over blocks on the back of your quilt or you can use them to make a bonus project.

"I cannot count my day complete 'til needle, thread and fabric meet."
        —Author Unknown

Introduction

5

Heart 2 Heart

Finished Quilt Size: 65" x 77"
Pieced by Brenda Bailey

Heart 2 Heart

65" x 77"
80 - 6" blocks

Fabric Needed:

Blocks	1 Layer Cake
Hearts	1/3 yard of 4 fabrics
Borders	1 1/3 yards
Fusible Web	1 1/2 yards
Binding	1/2 yard
Back	4 yards
Batting	69" x 81"

Designer's Notes

If I could, I would probably put a heart in every quilt I make. The heart is a simple shape, but there are so many patterns and variations used in quilting. When I saw this Layer Cake, I fell in love with the deep, rich reds and purples - they just seemed to beg to be hearts. Hence, this pattern. "My Heart Belongs to Daddy" is the name of my quilt because purple was my dad's favorite color. He passed away in 1999 and I miss him.

Brenda

Cutting Instructions:
Strips are cut selvage to selvage

1. Layer Cake
    Stack 4 Layer Cake squares and cut as in diagram.
    Repeat 10 times to cut 40 Layer Cake squares.
2. First Border
    Cut 6 - 2" strips from border fabric.
3. Middle Border
    Cut 1 - 3 1/2" strip from each heart fabric.
    Cut each strip into segments: 10 - 3 1/2".
4. Outside border
    Cut 7 - 4 1/2" strips from border fabric.

6 1/2" x 6 1/2"	3 1/2" x 6 1/2"
6 1/2" x 3 1/2"	3 1/2" x 3 1/2"

Cut 40

Sewing Instructions:
All seams are 1/4" - Press all seams

1. Hearts
    a. Make template of heart.
        Mark 80 hearts on smooth side of fusible web.
        You may want to cut out the center of the fusible web to avoid stiffness, leaving at least 1/4" inside the marked lines.
    b. Press 20 hearts on wrong side of each heart fabric.
        Cut out on lines.
    c. Divide up 3 1/2" x 6 1/2" Layer Cake pieces in 4 piles of 20, each pile having similar fabrics.
        (example: darks, lights or same colors together)
    d. Appliqué hearts - Match up 4 heart colors with 4 piles.
        Press hearts of one fabric onto Layer Cake pieces in pile 1.

Tip: Place bottom point of heart 1" from bottom of 3 1/2" x 6 1/2" piece.

7

Repeat for 3 remaining heart fabrics and 3 remaining piles.
Place piece of white paper behind Layer Cake fabric.
Finish edges of hearts using a close zig-zag.
Rip white paper from back.
Repeat to make 80.

2. Heart Blocks

    Stitch Color 1 heart piece to Color 2 heart piece, turning one heart upside down.
    Repeat to make 20.
    Stitch Color 3 heart piece to Color 4 heart piece, turning one heart upside down.
    Repeat to make 20.

Make 20

Make 20

Tip: Make sure that the same color hearts are all going in the same direction and are on the same side of the block.

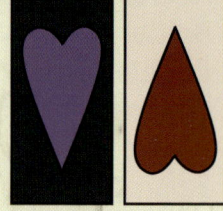

3. Construction

    Lay out 6 1/2" Layer Cake squares, alternately with heart blocks in 10 rows of 8.
    Stitch blocks together to make rows.
    Press away from heart blocks.
    Stitch rows together.

4. First Border - Press to border

    Stitch strips together end to end.
    Cut into segments: 2 - 60 1/2", 2 - 51 1/2".
    Stitch 60 1/2" pieces to right and left sides.
    Stitch 51 1/2" pieces to top and bottom.

5. Middle border - Press to first border

    (Uses 40 - 3 1/2" Layer Cake pieces and 40 - 3 1/2" heart fabric squares.)
    Stitch 21 - 3 1/2" squares together.
        Repeat to make 2.
    Stitch to right and left sides.
    Stitch 19 - 3 1/2" squares together.
        Repeat to make 2.
    Stitch to top and bottom.

Tip: Stitch 3 1/2" Layer Cake squares together alternately with 3 1/2" heart fabric squares.

6. Outside border - Press to outside border

    Stitch strips together end to end.
    Cut into segments: 2 - 69 1/2", 2 - 65 1/2".
    Stitch 69 1/2" pieces to right and left sides.
    Stitch 65 1/2" pieces to top and bottom.

7. Quilt and bind.

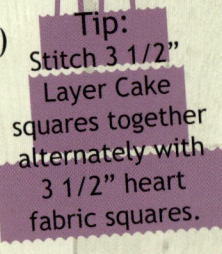

SUMMER SHERBET

```
2 qts. pineapple sherbet (softened)
1 lb. frozen strawberries
1/2 c. chopped walnuts
1 1/2 c. mini marshmallows
2 - 3 bananas (sliced)

Mix ingredients together and freeze.
```

Heart 2 Heart

Dash Away
Finished Quilt Size: 84" x 102"
Pieced by Bonnie Bailey

Dash Away

84" x 102"
70 - 7 1/2" Blocks

Fabric Needed:

Blocks	1 Layer Cake
Background	4 yards
Light Block Border	1 1/8 yards
Dark Block Border	1 3/4 yards
First and Outside Borders	1 1/3 yards
Binding	3/4 yard
Back	6 1/2 yards
Batting	88" x 106"

Designer's Notes

When we started designing patterns with 10" squares, I discovered that you could make a "positive" and a "negative" churn dash block using only one square and background fabric. I finally took the time to make the blocks, but when I got all of my blocks sewn together, I really struggled with how to lay them out. I wanted to put those two blocks together somehow. This is what evolved from many different layouts. The "dash" border is made to resemble a ribbon weaving in and out.

Bonnie

Cutting Instructions:
Strips are cut selvage to selvage

1. **Blocks**
   Stack 4 Layer Cake squares and cut as in diagram.
   Repeat 9 times to cut 35 Layer Cake squares.

   Cut 35

2. **Background**
   Cut 14 - 4" strips. Cut into segments: 140 - 4".
   Cut 16 - 2" strips. Cut into segments: 315 - 2".
   Cut 14 - 2" strips. (for ribbon border)
   Cut 7 - 2 1/2" strips. Cut into segments: 56 - 5". (for ribbon border)

3. **Dark Block Border**
   Cut 7 - 2" strips. (for ribbon border)
   Cut 26 - 1 1/2" strips.
      From 18 strips, cut segments: 36 - 17 1/2".
      From 8 strips, cut segments: 36 - 8".

4. **Light Block Border**
   Cut 22 - 1 1/2" strips.
      From each of 17 strips, cut segments: 2 - 15 1/2", 1 - 10".
      From 5 strips, cut segments: 17 - 10".

5. **First and Outside Borders**
   Cut 17 - 2 1/2" strips.
   Cut into segments: 2 - 98 1/2", 2 - 84". (for outside border)
   Cut into segments: 2 - 85 1/2", 2 - 71". (for first border)

Sewing Instructions:
All seams are 1/4" - Press all seams

1. **Block A**
   a. Half Square Triangles (HST)
      Mark diagonal lines on back of 70 - 4" background squares.

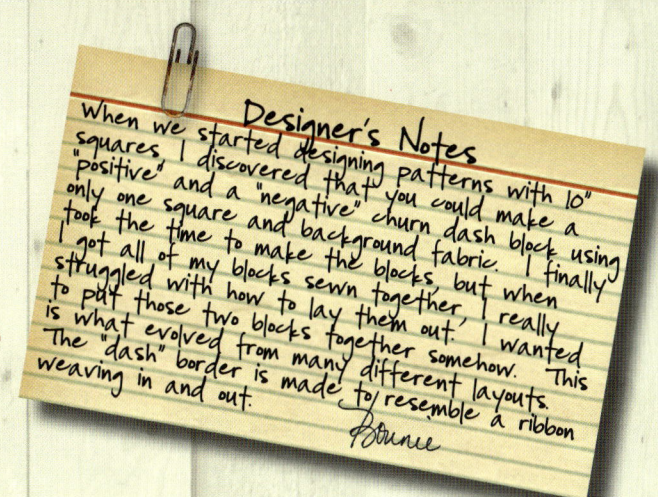

11

With right sides together (RST), lay marked squares on top of 4" Layer Cake squares.
Stitch 1/4" on both sides of diagonal lines.
Cut apart on lines.
Press to Layer Cake fabric.
Trim to 3 1/2" x 3 1/2". 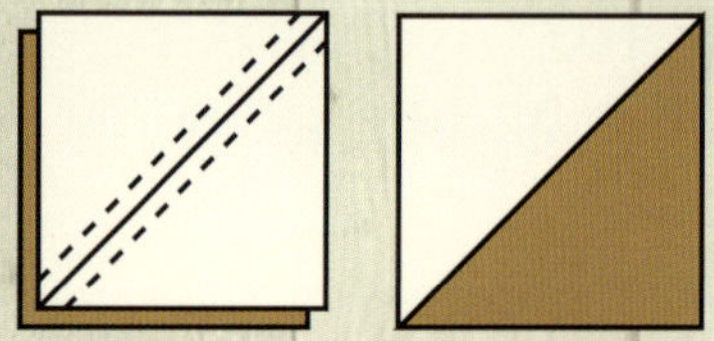
 b. Stitch 2" Layer Cake square to 2" background square.
  Repeat to make 4.
 c. Stitch 2" background square between 2 (b) units.
  Stitch (b) unit between 2 HST. Repeat to make 2.
  Stitch HST units to both sides of middle unit.
 Repeat to make 35 blocks - 1 from each Layer Cake fabric.

2. Block B
 a. Repeat (a) instructions from Block A.
 b. Repeat (b) instructions from Block A.
 c. Repeat (c) instructions from Block A using 2" Layer Cake piece in center in place of 2" background square.
 Repeat to make 35 blocks - 1 from each Layer Cake fabric.

3. Block Construction
 Stitch Block A to Block B of same Layer Cake fabric.
 Repeat to make 35.

4. Dark Block Border - Press to border
 Stitch 8" strips to top and bottom.
 Stitch 17 1/2" strips to right and left sides.
 Repeat to make 18.

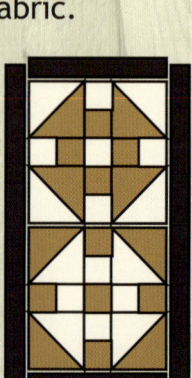

5. Light Block Border - Press to border
 Stitch 15 1/2" strips to right and left sides.
 Stitch 9 1/2" strips to top and bottom.
 Repeat to make 17.

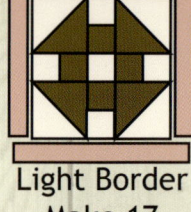

6. Construction
 Lay out blocks in 5 rows of 7, alternating border fabrics.
 Stitch blocks together in rows.
 Stitch rows together.

7. First Border - Press to border
 Stitch strips together end to end.
 Cut segments: 2 - 98 1/2", 2 - 85 1/2", 2 - 84", 2 - 71".
 Stitch 85 1/2" pieces to right and left sides.
 Stitch 71" pieces to top and bottom.
 Set aside 2 - 84" and 2 - 98 1/2" segments for outside border.

8. Ribbon Border - Press to first border
 Stitch 2" dark block border strip between 2 - 2" background strips. Press to dark.
 Repeat to make 7.
 Cut into segments: 56 - 4 1/2".
 Stitch 2 1/2" x 5" background pieces between 15 ribbon units.
  Repeat to make 2.
 Stitch to right and left sides. 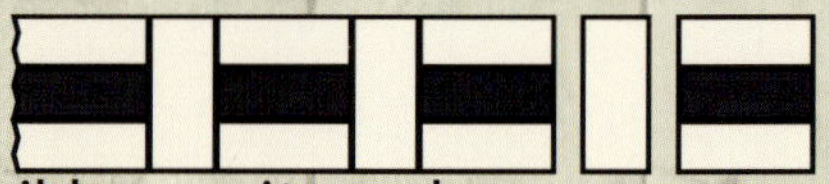
 Stitch 2 1/2" x 5" background pieces between 13 ribbon units and to both ends of border strip.

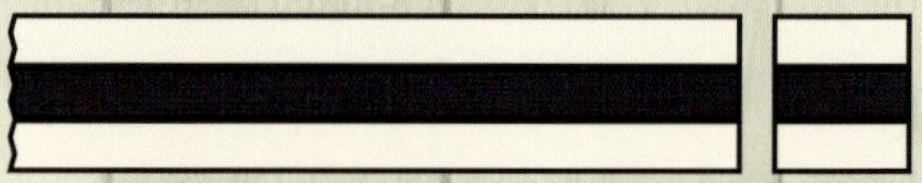

Block A
Make 35

Block B
Make 35

Dark Border
Make 18

Light Border
Make 17

Cut 56

Dash Away

12

Repeat to make 2.
Stitch to top and bottom.
9. Outside Border - Press to border
Stitch 98 1/2" pieces to right and left sides.
Stitch 84" pieces to top and bottom.
10. Quilt and bind.

GRANDMA BAILEY'S CARMEL ICE CREAM

4 c. sugar (divided)
2 quarts scalded milk
2 T. flour
pinch of salt
4 eggs - beaten
4 c. cream
2 T. vanilla

Measure 2 c. sugar into large heavy pan. Heat, stirring constantly until sugar becomes carmelized. Add scalded milk (milk will get big). Stir until carmel is dissolved. In separate bowl, mix 2 c. sugar, flour, salt and eggs. Pour slowly into milk mixture while whisking. Cool and add cream and vanilla. Freeze with ice cream freezer.

Dash Away

Arizona Trail

Finished Quilt Size: 63" x 72"
Pieced by Andrea Law

Arizona Trail

63" x 72"
156 - 4 1/2" Blocks

Fabric Needed:

Blocks	1 Layer Cake
Trail and Border	2 1/2 yards
Iron-on Interfacing	3 yards
Binding	1/2 yard
Back	4 yards
Batting	67" x 76"

Designer's Notes

I must give credit where it is due. Andrea Law from Page, AZ attended a lecture that I gave at a quilting retreat at Ruby's Inn. Each student was to come up with an idea for a layer cake design. We liked Andrea's idea so much that we asked if we could tweak it a little and use it for our book. She gave us permission and even pieced our model for us! We send out a great big heartfelt "Thanks" across the Arizona border to Andrea for her time and energy.

Bonnie

Cutting Instructions:
Strips are cut selvage to selvage

1. Trail and Border
    Cut 7 - 6 1/2" strips. Cut into segments: 40 - 6 1/2".
    Cut 8 - 5" strips. Cut 2 strips into segments: 4 - 9 1/2", 4 - 5".
       Set aside 6 strips for border.

Sewing Instructions:
All seams are 1/4" - Press all seams

1. Blocks
    a. Make template of circle.
    b. Mark 40 circles on smooth side of iron-on interfacing, leaving at least 1/2" between circles.
    c. Rough cut circles, leaving at least 1/4" around marked lines.
    d. Lay interfacing on right side of circle fabric with marked side up.
    e. Using a slightly smaller stitch, stitch on marked line, overlapping stitching about 1/2".
    f. Trim 1/8" outside of stitching.
    g. Slit interfacing and turn right side out.
    h. Push seams out with dull pencil and press, using a piece of toweling on ironing board.
    i. Center circle on Layer Cake square. Press into place.
    j. Finish edges of circle using matching or invisible thread.
    k. Cut out Layer Cake fabric and interfacing behind circle to remove bulk, leaving at least 1/4" inside of stitching.

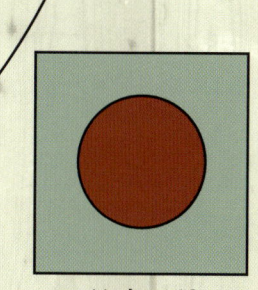

Make 40

Tip: Finishing stitches do not need to be close together because you have a finished edge.

1. Cut Layer Cake square into 4 - 5" squares as in diagram. Repeat with all 40 Layer Cake squares.

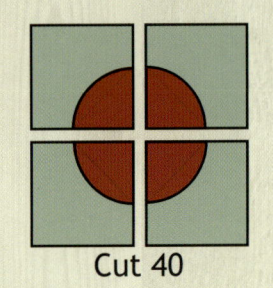

Cut 40

Tip: Measure Layer Cake squares carefully before cutting into 4 pieces. Do not assume that all squares are exactly 10" x 10".

2. Construction
   Lay out blocks in 14 rows of 12 with 5" x 9 1/2" pieces in corners taking place of 2 blocks.
   (There will be 4 blocks leftover)
   Stitch blocks together in rows.
   Stitch rows together.
3. Border - Press to border
   Stitch border strips together end to end.
   Cut into segments: 4 - 63 1/2".
   Stitch strips to right and left sides.
   Stitch strips to top and bottom.
4. Quilt and bind.

ANDREA LAW has been married 22 years and has 2 daughters. She lives in Page, Arizona on Lake Powell which is in the background of her picture. She named her quilt "Sandstone Garden" because the red reminds her of the sandstone there. She has lived in Page for 25 years and has been quilting for 15. Andrea is a very diversified quilter; she loves to try anything once. She has quilted everything from traditional to the very wild and crazy, but her favorite is appliqué.

Arizona Trail

Tip:
Experiment when laying your blocks out. There are lots of options, one of which is pictured here.

PEANUT BLOSSOMS

1/2 c. shortening
3/4 c. peanut butter
1/3 c. brown sugar
1/3 c. sugar
2 T. milk
1 egg
1 t. vanilla
1 1/2 c. flour
1 t. baking powder
1/2 t. salt
30 - 35 chocolate kisses

Unwrap kisses. In large bowl, cream shortening and peanut butter. Add sugars and beat until fluffy. Add egg, milk and vanilla. Beat well. Add flour, baking soda and salt to peanut butter mixture. Shape dough into balls. Roll in sugar. Place on ungreased cookie sheet. Bake at 375 degrees for 8 - 10 mins. Immediately place kisses on top of cookies, pressing down so cookie cracks around the edges.

Arizona Trail

17

Peas in a Pod

Finished Quilt Size: 42" x 54"
Pieced by Brenda Bailey

Misty Bailey   Autumn Oldroyd   Jesse Simmons

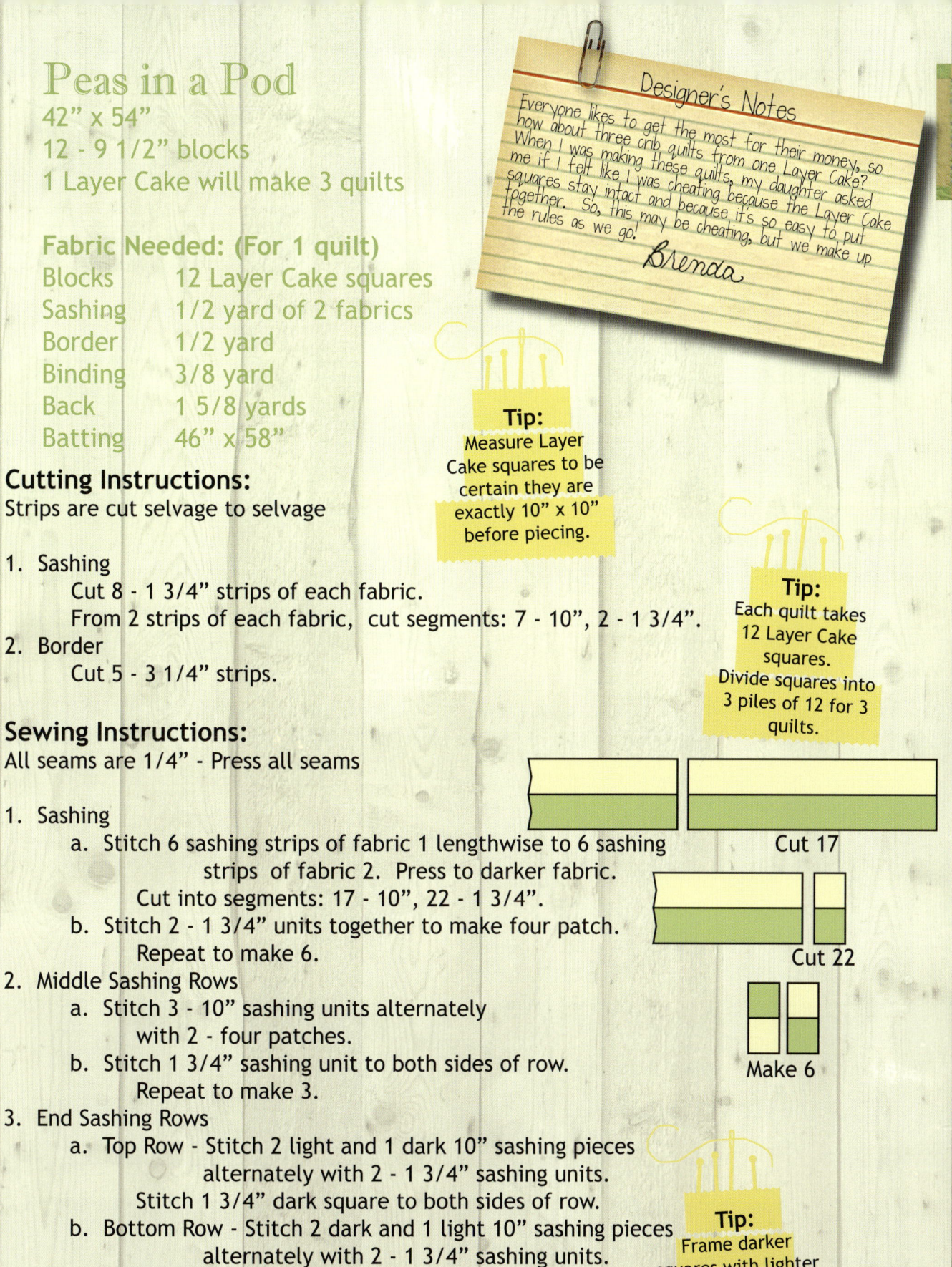

Peas in a Pod

42" x 54"
12 - 9 1/2" blocks
1 Layer Cake will make 3 quilts

Fabric Needed: (For 1 quilt)
Blocks   12 Layer Cake squares
Sashing   1/2 yard of 2 fabrics
Border   1/2 yard
Binding   3/8 yard
Back   1 5/8 yards
Batting   46" x 58"

Designer's Notes
Everyone likes to get the most for their money, so how about three crib quilts from one Layer Cake? When I was making these quilts, my daughter asked me if I felt like I was cheating because the Layer Cake squares stay intact and because it's so easy to put together. So, this may be cheating, but we make up the rules as we go!
Brenda

Tip: Measure Layer Cake squares to be certain they are exactly 10" x 10" before piecing.

Tip: Each quilt takes 12 Layer Cake squares. Divide squares into 3 piles of 12 for 3 quilts.

Cutting Instructions:
Strips are cut selvage to selvage

1. Sashing
   Cut 8 - 1 3/4" strips of each fabric.
   From 2 strips of each fabric, cut segments: 7 - 10", 2 - 1 3/4".
2. Border
   Cut 5 - 3 1/4" strips.

Sewing Instructions:
All seams are 1/4" - Press all seams

1. Sashing
   a. Stitch 6 sashing strips of fabric 1 lengthwise to 6 sashing strips of fabric 2. Press to darker fabric.
      Cut into segments: 17 - 10", 22 - 1 3/4".
   b. Stitch 2 - 1 3/4" units together to make four patch. Repeat to make 6.
2. Middle Sashing Rows
   a. Stitch 3 - 10" sashing units alternately with 2 - four patches.
   b. Stitch 1 3/4" sashing unit to both sides of row. Repeat to make 3.
3. End Sashing Rows
   a. Top Row - Stitch 2 light and 1 dark 10" sashing pieces alternately with 2 - 1 3/4" sashing units.
      Stitch 1 3/4" dark square to both sides of row.
   b. Bottom Row - Stitch 2 dark and 1 light 10" sashing pieces alternately with 2 - 1 3/4" sashing units.
      Stitch 1 3/4" light square to both sides of row.
4. Construction
   a. Lay out 12 Layer Cake squares in 4 rows of 3, alternating light and dark squares as best you can.

Cut 17

Cut 22

Make 6

Tip: Frame darker squares with lighter sashing and lighter squares with darker sashing.

19

b. Stitch blocks and sashing together to make rows.
　　　c. Stitch rows together.
5. Border - Press to border
　　　Stitch 3 strips together end to end.
　　　Cut into segments: 2 - 48 1/2".
　　　Cut remaining 2 strips into segments: 2 - 42".
　　　Stitch 48 1/2" strips to right and left sides.
　　　Stitch 42" strips to top and bottom.
6. Quilt and bind.

Tip:
You can combine the Layer Cake squares and make one larger quilt. Instructions included below.

Peas in a Pod
68" x 92"
35 - 9 1/2" Blocks

Fabric Needed:
Blocks	1 Layer Cake
Sashing	1 1/4 yard of 2 fabrics
Border	1 1/8 yards
Binding	2/3 yard
Back	5 1/2 yards
Batting	72" x 96"

Cutting Instructions:
Strips are cut selvage to selvage

1. Sashing
　　Lighter fabric - Cut 22 - 1 3/4" strips.
　　Cut 4 strips into segments: 14 - 10".
　　Darker fabric - Cut 21 - 1 3/4" strips.
　　Cut 3 strips into segments:
　　　　10 - 10", 4 - 1 3/4".
2. Border
　　Cut 8 - 4 1/4" strips.

Sewing Instructions:
All seams are 1/4" - Press all seams

1. Sashing
　　a. Stitch 18 sashing strips of fabric 1 lengthwise to 18 sashing strips of fabric 2. Press to darker fabric.
　　　Cut 15 into segments: 58 - 10".
　　　Cut 3 into segments: 68 - 1 3/4".
　　b. Stitch 2 - 1 3/4" units together to make four patch. Repeat to make 24.
2. Middle Sashing Rows
　　a. Stitch 5 - 10" sashing units alternately with 4 - four patches.

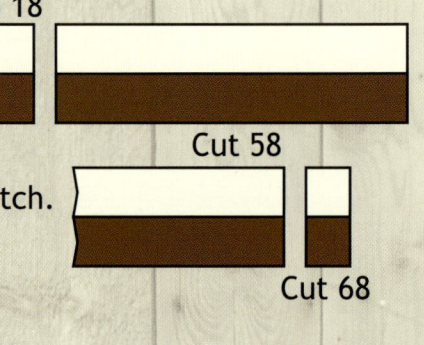

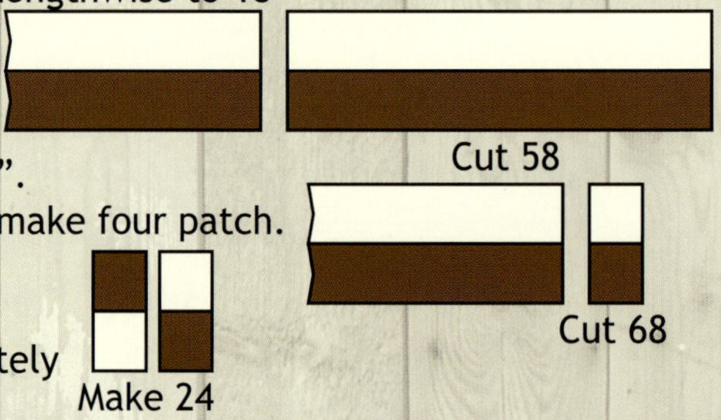

Cut 58
Cut 68
Make 24

    b. Stitch 1 3/4" sashing unit to both sides of row.
       Repeat to make 6.
3. End Sashing Rows
    a. Stitch 3 light and 2 dark 10" sashing pieces alternately with 4 - 1 3/4" sashing units.
    b. Stitch 1 3/4" dark square to both sides of row.
       Repeat to make 2.
4. Construction
    a. Lay out 35 Layer Cake squares in 7 rows of 5 alternating darks and lights as best you can.
    b. Stitch blocks and sashing together to make rows.
    c. Stitch rows together.
5. Border - Press to border
    Stitch strips together end to end.
    Cut into segments: 2 - 84 1/2", 2 - 68".
    Stitch 84 1/2" pieces to right and left sides.
    Stitch 68" pieces to top and bottom.
6. Quilt and bind.

BLUEBERRY BLISS

1 1/2 c. flour
1 T. sugar
1/2 t. salt
2 c. milk
2 eggs
1 t. vanilla
1 can blueberry pie filling
8 oz. cream cheese
4 oz. whipped topping
1/2 c. powdered sugar

Mix flour, sugar and salt. Add milk, eggs and vanilla. Mix well. Measure 1/4 c. batter into lightly buttered, hot pan and rotate pan until bottom is covered. Brown both sides. In separate bowl, mix cream cheese, whipped topping and powdered sugar. Fill each crêpe with cream cheese filling and roll up. Top with pie filling.

Peas in a Pod

Boston Commons
Finished Quilt Size: 77" x 90"
Pieced by Brenda Bailey

Boston Commons
77" x 90"

Fabric Needed:
Blocks	1 Layer Cake
Background	4 yards
Binding	2/3 yard
Back	5 yards
Batting	81" x 94"

Tip: This pattern can be made with 143 - 5" charm squares.

Designer's Notes
Every time I see a Boston Commons quilt, I am drawn to it. I'm not sure if it's because of the pattern or because it is a scrappy looking quilt. One morning while laying in bed, I began to wonder if I could make this pattern using a Layer Cake. I got up, did some figuring and found that it would work. I love the way it turned out! The extensive background gives ample room for beautiful quilting.
Brenda

Cutting Instructions:
Strips are cut selvage to selvage

1. Blocks
   Stack 4 Layer Cake squares and cut according to diagram.
   Repeat 9 times to cut 36 Layer Cake squares.
2. Background
   Cut 5 - 7 1/2" strips. Cut into segments: 24 - 7 1/2". (A)
       Cut each A square in half diagonally in both directions.
   Cut 2 - 7 5/8" squares. (B)
       Cut both B squares in half diagonally.
   Cut 2 - 4" squares. (C)
       Cut both C squares in half diagonally.
   Cut 5 - 10" strips. (for background border)
   Cut 8 - 4" strips. (for outside border)

Cut 36

A   B & C

Sewing Instructions:
All seams are 1/4" - Press all seams

1. Center Unit - Squares are 5" x 5" Layer Cake pieces
   a. Row 1
       Stitch 1 square between 2 (A) triangles.
       Repeat to make 2.
   b. Row 2
       Stitch 3 squares together.
       Stitch (A) triangles to both sides.
       Repeat to make 2.
   c. Row 3
       Stitch 5 squares together.
       Stitch (A) triangles to both sides.
       Repeat to make 2.
   d. Row 4
       Stitch 7 squares together.
       Stitch (A) triangles to both sides.
       Repeat to make 2.
   e. Row 5
       Stitch 9 squares together.
       Stitch (A) triangle to 1 side.
       Stitch (C) background triangle to opposite side.
       Repeat to make 2.

Tip: All background triangles will be larger than squares and will be trimmed later.

23

f. Row 6

  Stitch 9 squares together.

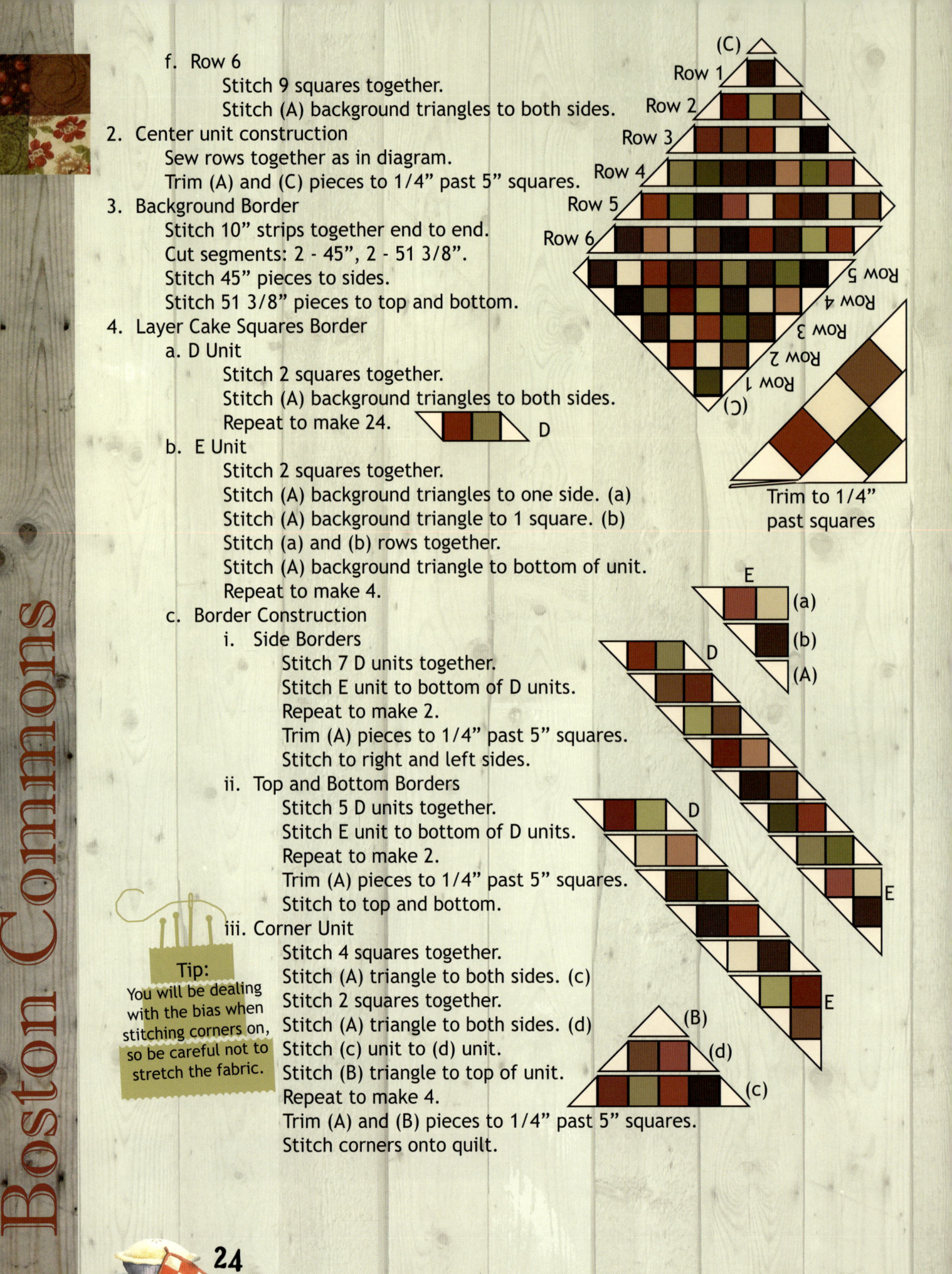

  Stitch (A) background triangles to both sides.

2. Center unit construction

  Sew rows together as in diagram.

  Trim (A) and (C) pieces to 1/4" past 5" squares.

3. Background Border

  Stitch 10" strips together end to end.

  Cut segments: 2 - 45", 2 - 51 3/8".

  Stitch 45" pieces to sides.

  Stitch 51 3/8" pieces to top and bottom.

4. Layer Cake Squares Border

  a. D Unit

    Stitch 2 squares together.

    Stitch (A) background triangles to both sides.

    Repeat to make 24.

  b. E Unit

    Stitch 2 squares together.

    Stitch (A) background triangles to one side. (a)

    Stitch (A) background triangle to 1 square. (b)

    Stitch (a) and (b) rows together.

    Stitch (A) background triangle to bottom of unit.

    Repeat to make 4.

  c. Border Construction

    i. Side Borders

      Stitch 7 D units together.

      Stitch E unit to bottom of D units.

      Repeat to make 2.

      Trim (A) pieces to 1/4" past 5" squares.

      Stitch to right and left sides.

    ii. Top and Bottom Borders

      Stitch 5 D units together.

      Stitch E unit to bottom of D units.

      Repeat to make 2.

      Trim (A) pieces to 1/4" past 5" squares.

      Stitch to top and bottom.

    iii. Corner Unit

      Stitch 4 squares together.

      Stitch (A) triangle to both sides. (c)

      Stitch 2 squares together.

      Stitch (A) triangle to both sides. (d)

      Stitch (c) unit to (d) unit.

      Stitch (B) triangle to top of unit.

      Repeat to make 4.

      Trim (A) and (B) pieces to 1/4" past 5" squares.

      Stitch corners onto quilt.

Tip: You will be dealing with the bias when stitching corners on, so be careful not to stretch the fabric.

Boston Commons

24

5. Outside Border
　　Stitch strips together end to end.
　　Cut into segments: 2 - 83 1/4", 2 - 77 1/2".
　　Stitch 83 1/4" pieces to right and left sides.
　　Stitch 77 1/2" pieces to top and bottom.
6. Quilt and bind.

BOSTON CREAM PIE

1 yellow cake mix
1 small cook and serve vanilla pudding
1 oz. unsweetened chocolate
3 T. butter   3/4 t. vanilla
1 c. powdered sugar   2 T. hot water

Cake: Prepare cake mix according to pkg. directions in 2 - 9" round cake pans.
Filling: Prepare pudding according to pkg. directions. Cool.
Chocolate glaze: Heat chocolate and butter over low heat until melted. Remove from heat and stir in powdered sugar and vanilla. Stir in water, one teaspoon at a time until glaze is desired consistency.
Assembly: Cover one cake round with filling. Place the other cake on filling. Glaze the top of the cake.

Boston Commons

25

Wall Flowers
Finished Quilt Size: 55" x 73"
Pieced by Bonnie Bailey

Wall Flowers
55" x 73"
35 - 9" Blocks

Fabric Needed:
Blocks	1 Layer Cake
First Border	1/2 yard
Outside Border	3/4 yard
Iron-on Interfacing	1 yard
Fusible Web	1/8 yard
Binding	1/2 yard
Back	3 1/3 yards
Batting	59" x 77"

Designer's Notes

I get excited about designs that have few seams to match up! And, almost as exciting: nearly every piece of the Layer Cake is used in this design. The flowers hide in the blocks like wall flowers (the kind I personified at high school dances) and the small flowers are cut out from behind the large flowers. You'll even use the leftovers from the flower blocks for the flowers' centers. Don't forget to try the super non-secret family recipe for Scotcheroos!

Bonnie

Cutting Instructions:
Strips are cut selvage to selvage

1. Block A
   Choose 10 Layer Cake squares that you want to be your flowers.
2. Block B
   Stack 4 Layer Cake squares and cut as in diagram.
   Repeat 5 times to cut 18 Layer Cake squares.
3. Block C
   Stack 4 Layer Cake squares and cut as in diagram.
   Repeat 3 times to cut 12 Layer Cake squares.
4. First Border
   Cut 6 - 2 1/2" strips.
5. Outside Border
   Cut 6 - 3 1/2" strips.

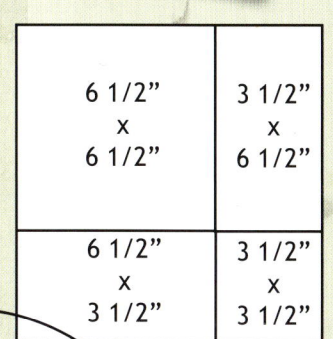

6 1/2" x 6 1/2"	3 1/2" x 6 1/2"
6 1/2" x 3 1/2"	3 1/2" x 3 1/2"

Cut 18

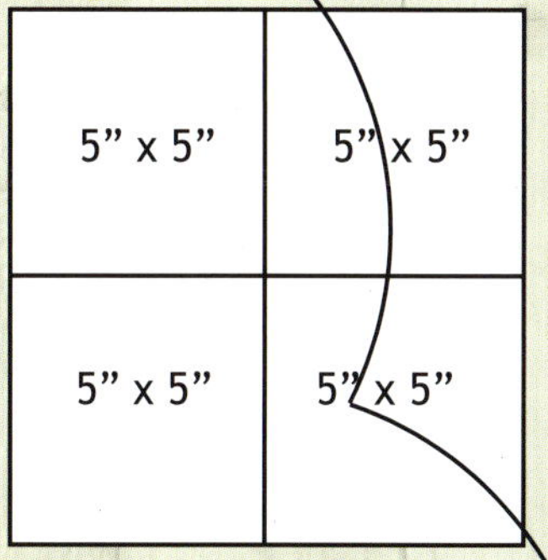

5" x 5"	5" x 5"
5" x 5"	5" x 5"

Cut 12

Sewing Instructions:
1. Block A
   a. Make template of large flower and flower center.
   b. Mark 5 flowers on smooth side of iron-on interfacing, leaving at least 1/2" between flowers.
   c. Rough cut flowers, leaving at least 1/4" around marked lines.
   d. Lay interfacing on right side of Layer Cake square (from pile of 10) with marked side up.
   e. Using a slightly smaller stitch, stitch on marked line, overlapping stitching about 1/2".
   f. Trim to 1/8" outside of stitching.
   g. Slit interfacing and turn right side out.
   h. Push edges out with dull pencil and press, using a piece of toweling on ironing board.
   i. Center flower on Layer Cake square (from pile of 10). Press into place.

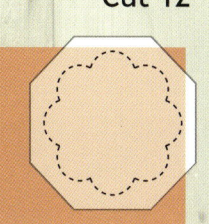

j. Finish edges of flower using matching or invisible thread.
k. Cut out Layer Cake fabric and interfacing behind flowers leaving at least 1/4" inside stitching. (Small flowers are made from these pieces, so cut carefully around edge to leave piece big enough for small flower.)
l. Mark 5 large flower centers on smooth side of fusible web. Press circles on wrong side of fabric leftover from large flowers.
Cut out on lines.
Center circles on flowers and press into place.
Finish edges of circles using a close zig-zag.
Repeat to make 5.
Trim blocks to 9 1/2" x 9 1/2".

Block A Make 5

Tip: Finishing stitches on flowers do not need to be close together because you have a finished edge.

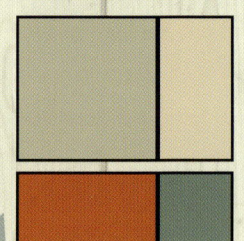

Block B Make 18

2. Block B
   a. Block Construction
      Stitch 6 1/2" square to 3 1/2" x 6 1/2" piece.
      Press to square.
      Stitch 3 1/2" square to 3 1/2" x 6 1/2" piece.
      Press to square.
      Stitch units together.
      Repeat to make 18.
   b. Appliquéd Block
      Choose 5 B blocks on which to appliqué small flower.
      Make template of small flower and flower center.
      Follow instructions for Block A (b - l) using piece cut from behind large flower to make small flower.
      Repeat to make 5.

Block B(b) (use 5 from 18 above)

3. Block C
   Stitch 2 - 5" squares together.
   Repeat to make 24.
   Stitch 2 units together.
   Repeat to make 12.
4. Construction
   Lay out blocks in 7 rows of 5.
   Stitch blocks together in rows.
   Stitch rows together.
5. First Border - Press to border
   Stitch strips together end to end.
   Cut into segments: 2 - 63 1/2", 2 - 49 1/2".
   Stitch 63 1/2" strips to right and left sides.
   Stitch 49 1/2" strips to top and bottom.
6. Outside Border - Press to border
   Stitch strips together end to end.
   Cut into segments: 2 - 67 1/2", 2 - 55 1/2".
   Stitch 67 1/2" strips to right and left sides.
   Stitch 55 1/2" strips to top and bottom.
7. Quilt and bind.

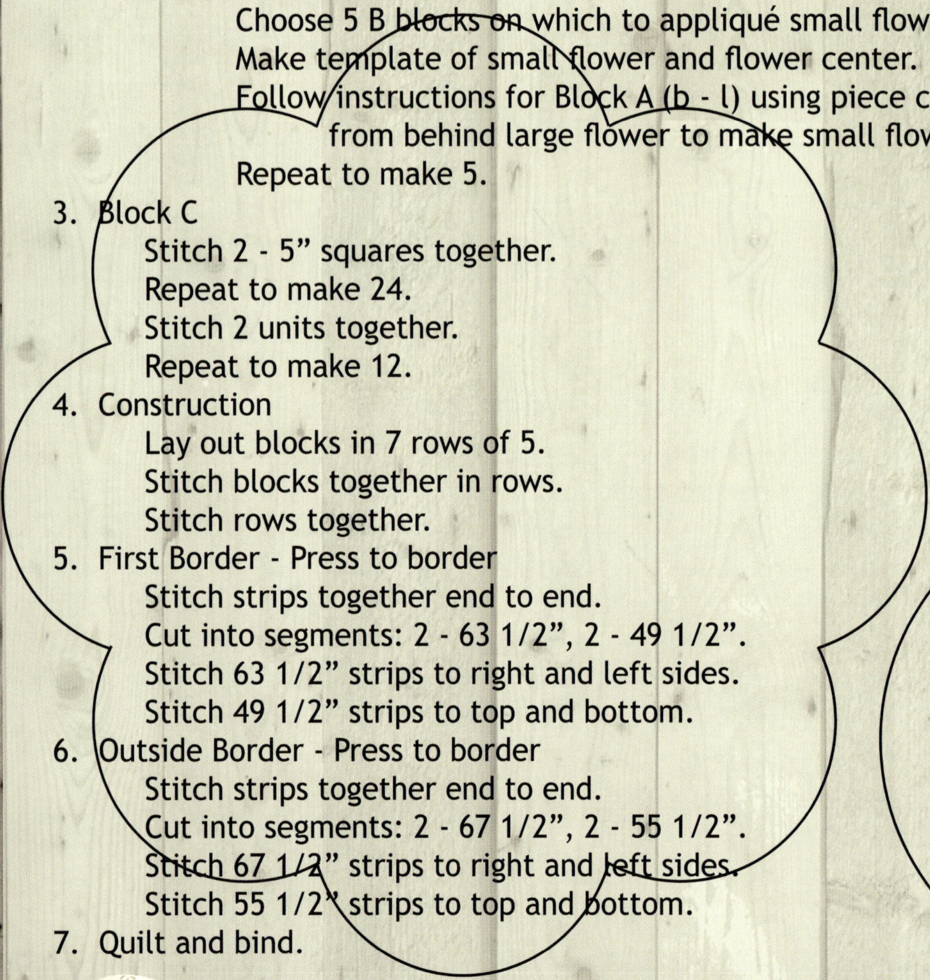

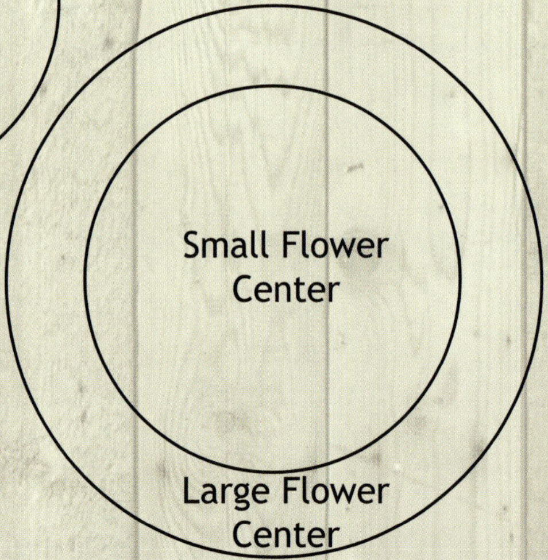

Block C Make 12

Small Flower Center

Large Flower Center

Wall Flowers

SCOTCHEROOS

- 6 c. rice krispies cereal
- 1 c. sugar
- 1 c. light corn syrup
- 1 c. peanut butter
- 1 c. chocolate chips
- 1 c. butterscotch chips

Measure cereal into large bowl. In medium sauce pan, cook sugar and corn syrup. Bring to boil and stir in peanut butter. Add peanut butter mixture to cereal and mix to coat. Press mixture into 9 x 13 pan • Melt chocolate chips and butterscotch chips together and spread on top. Cool and cut into bars.

Wall Flowers

Final Four

Finished Quilt Size: 84" x 97"
Pieced by Bonnie Bailey

Final Four

84" x 97"
30 - 13" blocks

Fabric Needed:

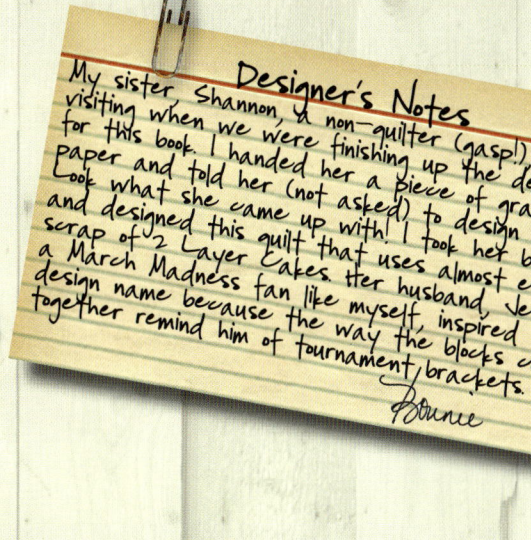

Blocks	2 Layer Cakes
First & Third Borders	1 yard
Outside Border	1 3/8 yards
Binding	3/4 yard
Back	6 1/2 yards
Batting	88" x 101"

Designer's Notes

My sister Shannon, a non-quilter (gasp!), was visiting when we were finishing up the designs for this book. I handed her a piece of graph paper and told her (not asked) to design a block. Look what she came up with! I took her block and designed this quilt that uses almost every scrap of 2 Layer Cakes. Her husband, Jeff, a March Madness fan like myself, inspired the design name because the way the blocks come together remind him of tournament brackets.

Bonnie

Cutting Instructions:

Strips are cut selvage to selvage

1. Blocks - *pieces will be used in border
   a. Stack 4 Layer Cake squares and cut as in diagram.
      Repeat 8 times to cut 32 Layer Cake squares.
   b. Stack 4 Layer Cake squares and cut as in diagram.
      Repeat 2 times to cut 8 Layer Cake squares.
   c. Stack 4 Layer Cake squares and cut as in diagram.
      Repeat 5 times to cut 18 Layer Cake squares.
   d. Stack 4 Layer Cake squares and cut as in diagram.
      Repeat 6 times to cut 22 Layer Cake squares.
2. First & Third Borders
   Cut 16 - 2" strips.
3. Outside Border
   Cut 9 - 5" strips.

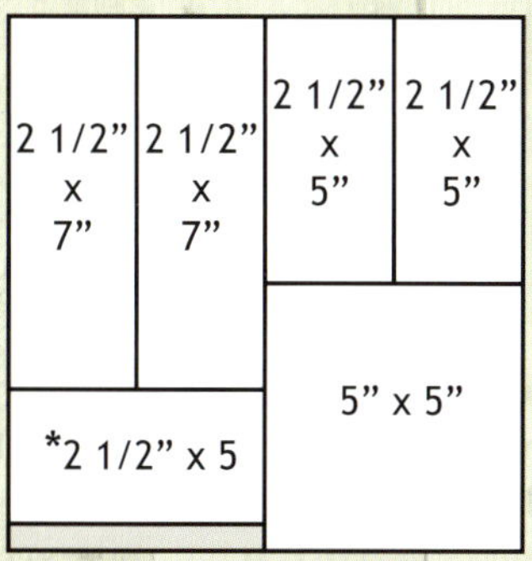

(a) Cut 32
(b) Cut 8 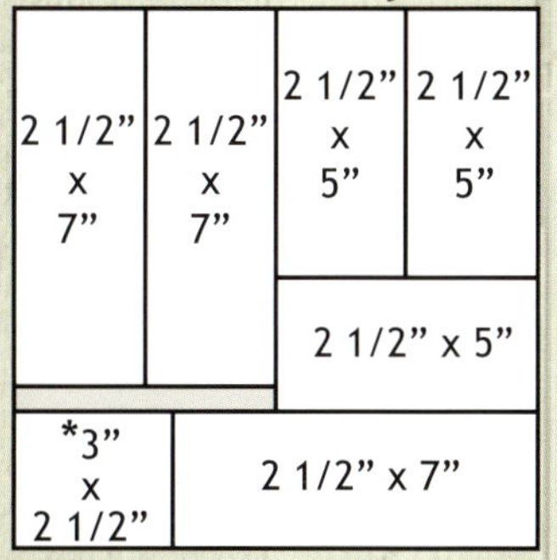
(c) Cut 18 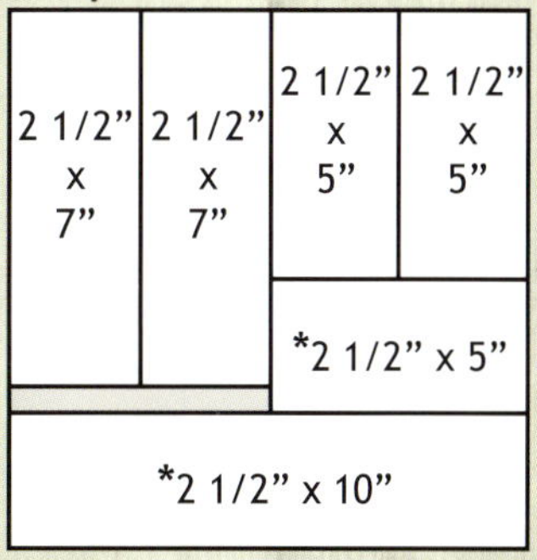
(d) Cut 22 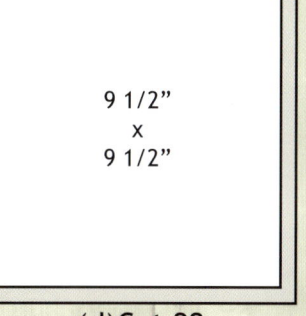

Sewing Instructions:

All seams are 1/4" - Press all seams

1. Block A
   a. Stitch 2 - 2 1/2" x 5" (2 different fabrics) Layer Cake
         pieces together end to end.
      Repeat with same 2 fabrics.
      Stitch to opposite sides of 9 1/2" Layer Cake square.
   b. Using same 2 fabrics, stitch 2 - 2 1/2" x 7" Layer Cake
         pieces together end to end.
      Repeat to make 2.
      Stitch to remaining 2 sides of Layer Cake square.
      Repeat to make 22.

Block A 
Make 22

31

2. Block B
   a. Stitch 2 - 5" x 5" Layer Cake pieces together.
      Repeat to make 16.
      Set 4 units aside to use in Block C.
      Stitch 2 units together to make four patch.
      Repeat to make 6.
   b. Stitch 2 - 2 1/2" x 5" Layer Cake pieces
      together end to end.
      Repeat with same 2 fabrics.
      Stitch to opposite sides of four patch.
   c. Using same 2 fabrics, stitch 2 - 2 1/2" x 7" Layer Cake
      pieces together end to end.
      Repeat to make 2.
      Stitch to remaining 2 sides of four patch.
      Repeat to make 6.
3. Block C
   a. Stitch 2 1/2" x 5" Layer Cake pieces to sides of two
      square unit that was set aside in Block B
      instructions.
   b. Stitch 2 - 2 1/2" x 7" pieces together end to end.
      Stitch to top of two square unit.
      Repeat to make 4.
4. Construction
   Lay out blocks in 5 rows of 6, offsetting rows 2 and 4 by
      stitching Block C to both sides.
   Stitch blocks together to make rows.
   Stitch rows together.
5. First Border - Press to border
   Stitch strips together end to end.
   Cut into segments: 2 - 78 1/2", 2 - 68 1/2".
   Set aside remaining border strips for third border.
   Stitch 68 1/2" pieces to right and left sides.
   Stitch 78 1/2" pieces to top and bottom.
6. Pieces Border - Press to first border
   Stitch leftover 2 1/2" Layer Cake pieces
      together end to end.
   Cut into segments: 2 - 81 1/2", 2 - 72 1/2".
   Stitch 72 1/2" pieces to right and left sides.
   Stitch 81 1/2" pieces to top and bottom.
7. Third Border - Press to border
   Using strips from first border, cut into segments:
      2 - 85 1/2", 2 - 75 1/2".
   Stitch 75 1/2" pieces to right and left sides.
   Stitch 85 1/2" pieces to top and bottom.
8. Outside Border - Press to border
   Stitch strips together end to end.
   Cut into segments: 2 - 88 1/2", 2 - 84 1/2".
   Stitch 84 1/2" pieces to right and left sides.
   Stitch 88 1/2" pieces to top and bottom.
9. Quilt and bind.

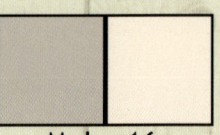

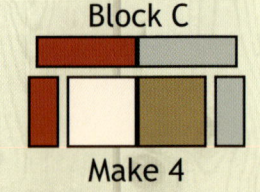

Make 16

Block B
Make 6

Block C
Make 4

CHOCOLATE FOUR DESSERT

1 pkg. Oreo cookies
6 T. margarine
8 oz. cream cheese
1/2 c. powdered sugar
1 large instant chocolate pudding
2 c. milk
12 oz. whipped topping

Crush 3/4 pkg. Oreos and mix with melted margarine. Press into 9 x 13 pan. Mix cream cheese, 1/2 container whipped topping and powdered sugar until creamy. Spread on top of Oreo mixture. Mix pudding with milk. Spread on top of cream cheese mixture. Spread remaining whipped topping on top of pudding. Crumble remaining cookies on top.

33

Slice & Dice

Finished Quilt Size: 68" x 92"
Pieced by Brenda Bailey

Slice & Dice

68" x 92"
35 - 12" blocks

Fabric Needed:

Blocks	1 Layer Cake
Background	2 2/3 yards
Block Borders	5/8 yard of 5 fabrics
Border	1 1/8 yards
Binding	2/3 yard
Back	5 yards
Batting	72" x 96"

Designer's Notes

Do you shy away from patterns that include curves? Well, this is an easy way to make a curved seam because it's appliqued! This pattern may look difficult, but once you get that curve figured out, it goes together easily. We called the design "Slice and Dice" because it looks like slices of fruit. I'm excited to see what fabrics you choose because this pattern would be darling using any Layer Cake.

Brenda

Cutting Instructions:

Strips are cut selvage to selvage

1. **Blocks**
   Make template of curved piece. (page 36)
   Cut 35 Layer Cake squares as in diagram.
2. **Background**
   Cut 18 - 5" strips.
   Cut into segments: 140 - 5".
3. **Block Borders**
   From each fabric: Cut 1 - 5" strip.
   Cut into segments: 28 - 1 1/4" bias strips.
   From each fabric: Cut 5 - 2" strips.
   Cut into segments: 14 - 12 1/2".
   From each fabric: Cut 4 - 1" strips.
   Cut into segments: 28 - 4 3/4", 7 - 1".
4. **Border**
   Cut 8 - 4 1/2" strips.

Sewing Instructions:

All seams are 1/4" - Press all seams

1. **Curves**
   Lay curved piece on 5" background square.
   Press bias piece in half lengthwise.
   Lay raw edges of bias strip on curved edge. Stitch *scant* 1/4" from raw edge, making sure the bias strip is doubled where you stitch. The ends of the bias strip will extend over the edges.
   Turn and press bias strip. Spray with water if necessary to get it to lay flat.

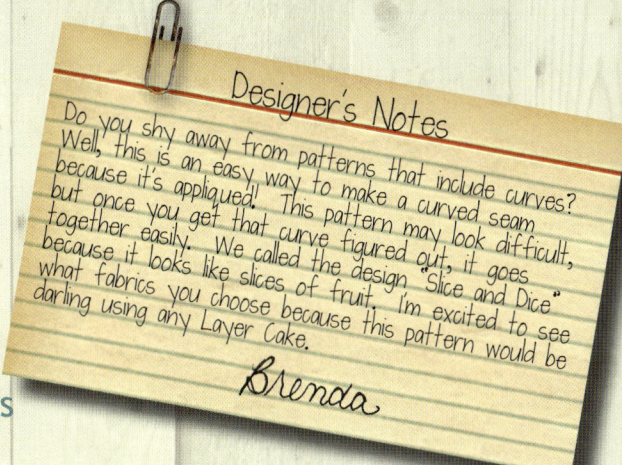

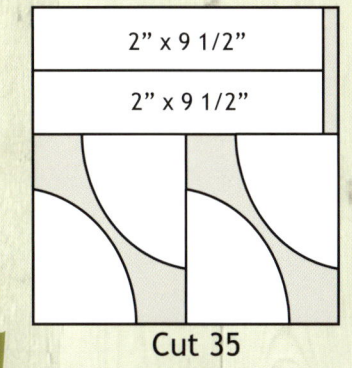

Cut 35

Tip: Cut all curved pieces in the same direction.

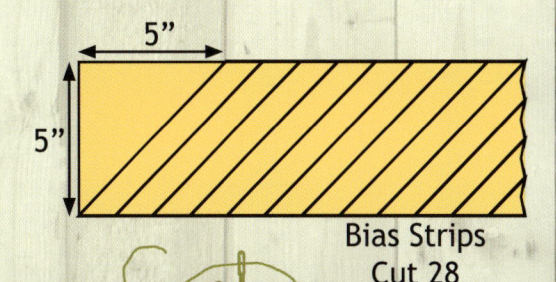

Bias Strips
Cut 28

Tip: When stitching, don't pull the bias strip, but ease it in as you stitch around the curve.

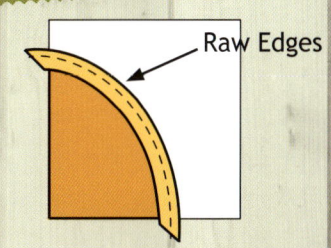

Raw Edges

35

Top stitch folded edge of bias strip.
Press and spray if necessary.
Trim square to 4 3/4" x 4 3/4", leaving the same distance past the small part of the curve on all blocks (about 1/2").
Repeat to make 140, using the same color bias on all 4 curved pieces of the same fabric.

Make 140

2. Block Construction
   Stitch 1" strip between 2 curve squares of the same fabric.
   Press to strip.
   Repeat to make 2.
   Stitch 1" square between 2 - 1" strips. Press to strips.
   Stitch between 2 curved units.
   Repeat to make 35 blocks.
3. Block Borders - Press to border
   Stitch 2 matching Layer Cake strips to right and left sides.
   Stitch 2 - 2" x 12 1/2" matching block border fabric strips to top and bottom.
   Repeat to make 35.
4. Construction
   Lay out blocks in 7 rows of 5, turning every other block.
   Stitch blocks together in rows.
   Stitch rows together.
5. Border - Press to border
   Stitch strips together end to end.
   Cut into segments: 2 - 84 1/2", 2 - 68 1/2".
   Stitch 84 1/2" pieces to right and left sides.
   Stitch 68 1/2" pieces to top and bottom.
6. Quilt and bind.

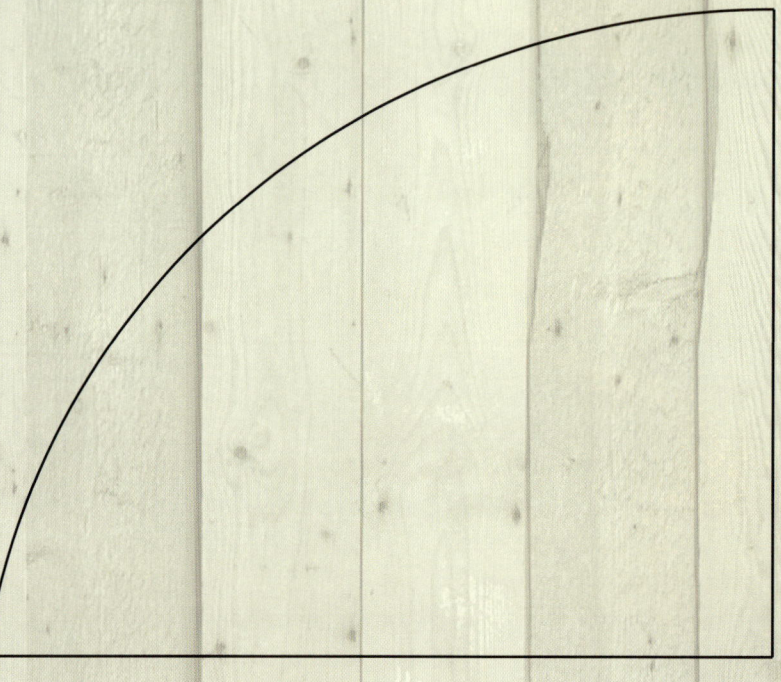

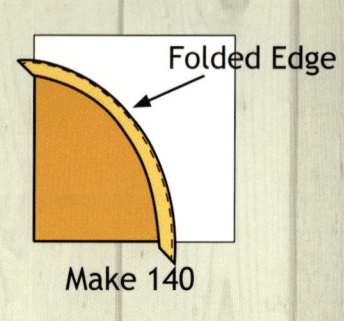

Make 35

BUSY DAY LEMON CHEESECAKE

8 oz. cream cheese (softened)
2 c. milk
1 small instant lemon pudding
8" graham cracker crust

Stir cream cheese until creamy. Blend in 1/2 c. milk. Add remaining milk and pudding. Beat slowly with hand mixer just until well mixed (about 1 min. - do not overbeat). Pour into graham cracker crust. Chill before serving.

Slice & Dice

37

Simple Simon

Finished Quilt Size: 56" x 76"
Pieced by Bonnie Bailey

Simple Simon

56" x 76"
25 - 9" x 13" blocks

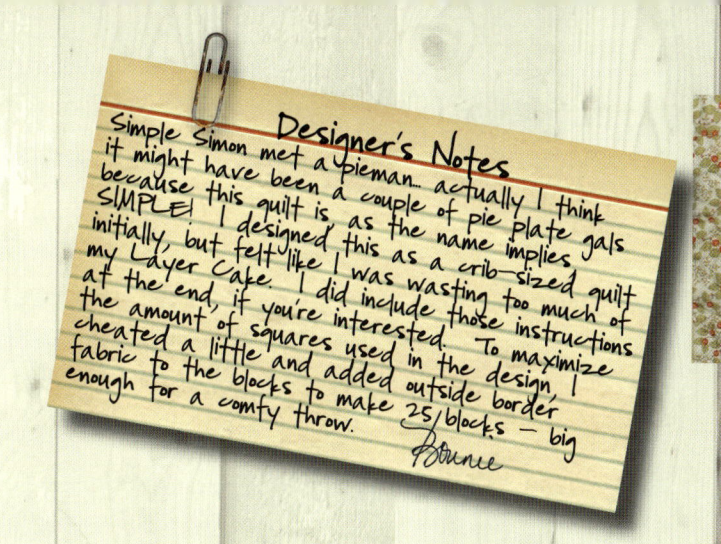

Fabric Needed:

Blocks	1 Layer Cake
Sashing	1 yard
Border	3/4 yard
Binding	1/2 yard
Back	3 1/2 yards
Batting	60" x 80"

Designer's Notes

Simple Simon met a pieman... actually I think it might have been a couple of pie plate gals because this quilt is as the name implies SIMPLE! I designed this as a crib-sized quilt initially, but felt like I was wasting too much of my Layer Cake. I did include those instructions at the end, if you're interested. To maximize the amount of squares used in the design, I cheated a little and added outside border fabric to the blocks to make 25 blocks - big enough for a comfy throw.
Bonnie

Cutting Instructions:
Strips are cut selvage to selvage

1. Blocks
    Stack 4 Layer Cake squares and cut as in diagram.
    Repeat 4 times to cut 16 Layer Cake squares.
2. Block Borders
    Stack 4 Layer Cake squares and cut as in diagram.
    Repeat 6 times to cut 24 Layer Cake squares.
3. Sashing
    Cut 19 - 1 1/2" strips.
    Cut 13 strips into segments: 20 - 13 1/2",
        20 - 9 1/2", 16 - 1 1/2".
    Reserve 6 strips for first border.
4. Outside Border
    Cut 7 - 3" strips. Cut into segments: 2 - 10". (for blocks)
    Reserve the rest of the strips for the border.
    Cut 1 - 2 1/2" strip.
    Cut into segments: 4 - 9 1/2". (for blocks)

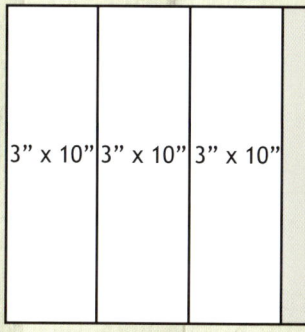

Tip: Remember to include border pieces (for blocks) along with Layer Cake pieces in sewing instructions 1 & 2.

Blocks Cut 16 — 3" x 10", 3" x 10", 3" x 10"

Block Borders Cut 24 — 2 1/2" x 9 1/2", 2 1/2" x 9 1/2", 2 1/2" x 9 1/2", 2 1/2" x 9 1/2"

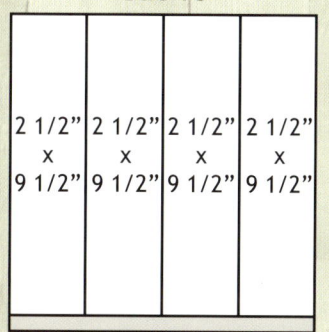

Sewing Instructions:
All seams are 1/4" - Press all seams

1. Blocks
    Stitch 2 - 3" x 10" Layer Cake pieces together lengthwise.
    Cut unit perpendicular to the seam into 2 - 5" pieces.
    Turn one unit and stitch back together.
    Repeat to make 25.
2. Block Borders - Press to border
    Stitch 2 1/2" x 9 1/2" Layer Cake pieces to right and
        left sides.
    Stitch 2 1/2" x 9 1/2" Layer Cakes pieces to top and
        bottom.
    Repeat to make 25.

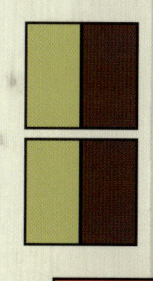

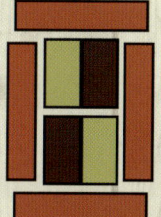

Make 25

3. Lay blocks out in 5 rows of 5.
4. Sashing - Press to sashing
    a. Stitch 4 - 13 1/2" sashing pieces between 5 blocks to make row.
       Repeat to make 5 rows.
    b. Stitch 4 - 1 1/2" sashing squares between 5 - 9 1/2" sashing pieces to make sashing row.
       Repeat to make 4 sashing rows.
    c. Stitch sashing rows between block rows.
5. First Border - Press to border
    Stitch 6 sashing strips together end to end.
        Cut into segments: 2 - 69 1/2", 2 - 51 1/2".
    Stitch 69 1/2" pieces to right and left sides.
    Stitch 51 1/2" pieces to top and bottom.
6. Outside Border - Press to border
    Stitch strips together end to end.
    Cut into segments: 2 - 71 1/2", 2 - 56 1/2".
    Stitch 71 1/2" pieces to right and left sides.
    Stitch 56 1/2" pieces to top and bottom.
7. Quilt and bind.

Simple Simon

Finished Quilt Size: 41" x 57"

Tip: Simple Simon can easily be modified to make a smaller quilt by changing the cutting directions and omitting the outside border.

Cutting Instructions:
Refer to page 39

1. Blocks
   Cut 11 as in diagram.
2. Block Borders
   Cut 16 as in diagram.
3. Sashing
   Cut 12 - 1 1/2" strips.
   Cut 7 strips into segments:
   12 - 13 1/2", 12 - 9 1/2", 9 - 1 1/2".
   Reserve 5 strips for border.
4. Border
   Sew strips end to end.
   Cut into segments: 2 - 55 1/2", 2 - 41 1/2".

Sewing Instructions:
Refer to page 39 - 40

Follow sewing instructions 1 - 7 making only 16 blocks - 4 rows of 4.

PENNY PIE

1 unbaked pie crust
1 c. shortening
1/2 c. sugar
1 c. brown sugar
1 t. vanilla
2 eggs
2 1/4 c. flour
1 t. soda
1 t. salt
2 c. chocolate chips

Cream sugars and eggs. Add remaining ingredients. Fill pie crust with dough. Bake at 375 degrees for 30 mins. or until golden brown. Serve in small slices.

Simple Simon

Yours Truly
Finished Quilt Size: 68" x 87"
Pieced by Brenda Bailey

Yours Truly
68" x 87"
48 - 9 1/2" blocks

Fabric Needed:
Blocks   1 Layer Cake
Background   1 1/3 yards
Cherries   1/8 yard of 2 fabrics
Stems   1/4 yard
Leaves   1/4 yard
First Border   3/8 yard
Outside Border   1 1/4 yards
Fusible Web   1 yard
Binding   2/3 yard
Back   5 yards
Batting   72" x 91"

Designer's Notes
This pattern has endless possibilities. I modified a motif from the fabrics in my quilts to make my appliqué designs. To personalize your quilt, you could do the same, or appliqué your favorite design. Instead of appliqué, you could fussy cut these blocks or even use your family photos. With all of these options, you can use this pattern to make a quilt that is yours, truly!

Brenda

Cutting Instructions:
Strips are cut selvage to selvage

1. Blocks
    Stack 4 Layer Cake squares and cut as in diagram.
    Repeat 4 times to cut 16 Layer Cake squares.
2. Background
    Cut 5 - 8 1/2" strips. Cut into segments: 24 - 8 1/2".
        (will trim later)
3. First Border
    Cut 7 - 1 1/2" strips.
4. Outside Border
    Cut 8 - 5" strips.

[Diagram: 6 strips of 1 1/2" x 9"]
Cut 16

Sewing Instructions:
All seams are 1/4" – Press all seams

1. Cherry Blocks
    a. Make templates for cherry, stem and leaf. (page 46)
    b. Mark 48 cherries, 24 stems and 48 leaves
        on smooth side of fusible web.
    c. Arrange stem, cherries and leaves on
        8 1/2" background square.
    d. Press stem into place.
    e. Place white paper behind background fabric to act
        as a stabilizer and zig-zag around stem.

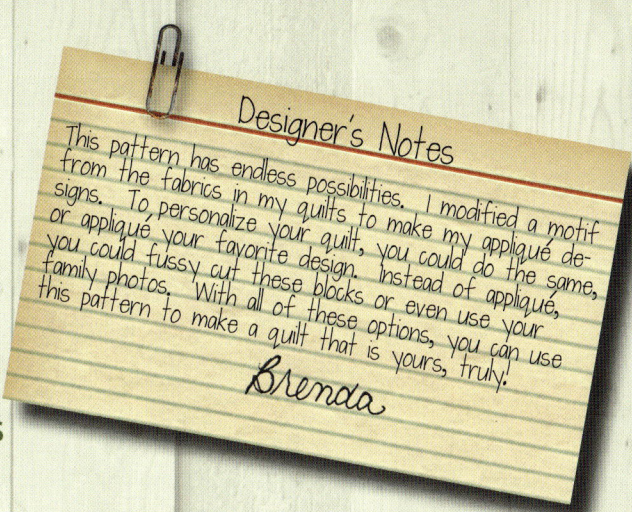

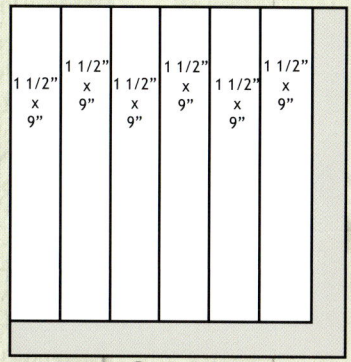

Tip:
Since this is raw-edge appliqué, close stitching works best.

f. Press cherries and leaves into place.
g. Zig-zag around cherries and leaves.
h. Rip white paper from back.
    Repeat to make 24.
    Trim blocks to 8" x 8".
2. Cherry Block Border - Press to border after each seam
    a. Using 4 - 1 1/2" x 9" Layer Cake pieces, stitch 1 strip to top
        of block, ending stitching 2" from the edge.
    b. Stitch 1 1/2" x 9" strip to right side.
    c. Stitch 1 1/2" x 9" strip to bottom.
    d. Stitch 1 1/2" x 9" strip to left side.
    e. Stitch remainder of first strip.
        Repeat to make 24.
3. Construction
    Lay out cherry blocks alternately with
        10" Layer Cake squares in 8 rows of 6.
    Stitch blocks together in rows.
    Press to Layer Cake squares.
    Stitch rows together.
4. First border - Press to border
    Stitch strips together end to end.
    Cut into segments:
        2 - 76 1/2", 2 - 59 1/2".
    Stitch 76 1/2" pieces to
        right and left sides.
    Stitch 59 1/2" pieces
        to top and bottom.
5. Outside border - Press to border
    Stitch strips together
        end to end.
    Cut into segments:
        2 - 78 1/2", 2 - 68 1/2".
    Stitch 78 1/2" pieces to
        right and left sides.
    Stitch 68 1/2" pieces to
        top and bottom.
6. Quilt and bind.

Tip: Measure Layer Cake squares to be certain they are exactly 10" x 10" before piecing.

Make 24

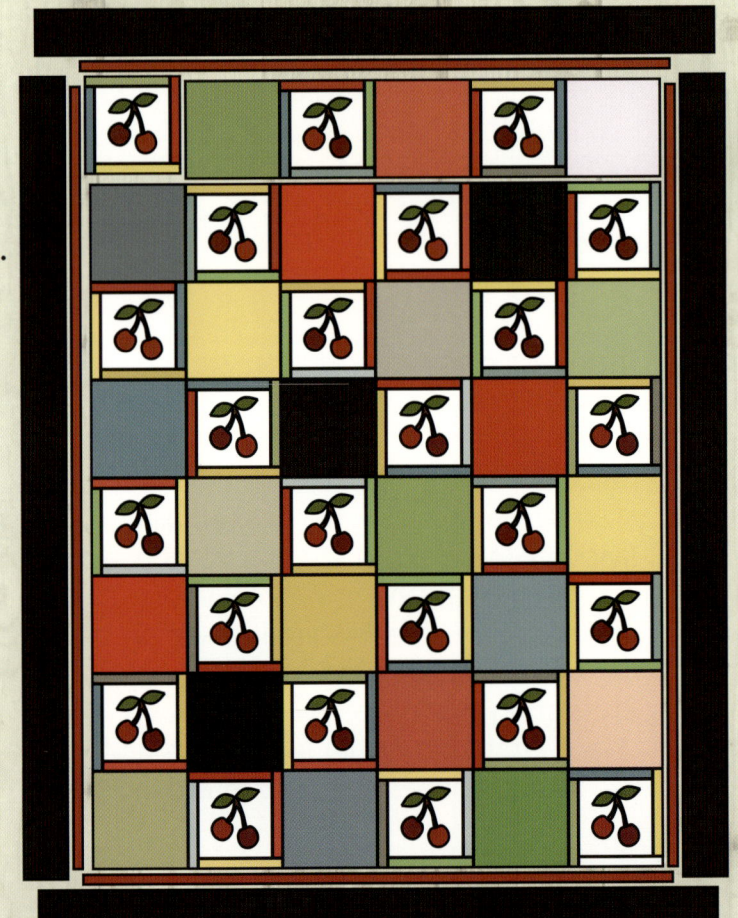

Tip:
Make this quilt yours, truly with your choice of appliqué shape. (flower and car included on page 46)

CHERRY CHOCOLATE CAKE

1 devil's food cake mix
1 can cherry pie filling
3 eggs
Mix together until well blended.
Pour into 9 x 13 pan. Bake at 350 degrees for 25 – 35 mins.

Frosting:
1 c. sugar
1/3 c. milk
5 T. butter
1 c. chocolate chips
Mix sugar, milk and butter together in sauce pan. Heat until bubbly. Remove from heat and add chocolate chips. Stir thoroughly. Frost cake when cool.

45

Yours Truly

Cherry Leaf

Cherry Stem

Flower Center

Tip: Shapes will be reversed when appliqué is complete.

Cherry

Yours Truly

46

The Alan & Brenda Bailey Family 2008
Bonnie, Ross, Matt
Alice, Shannon, Brenda, Alan, Laurel, Holly

The Alan & Brenda Bailey Family 1992
From Left: Holly, Shannon, Bonnie,
Matt, Brenda, Laurel, Alice, Alan, Ross

BRENDA BAILEY

Mix 1 c. common sense with sweet gal who went to school with nearly everyone. Let rise. Add in 1 college education and Jr. High teaching experience. After 1 year, mix in 1 tall cowboy and move to small country town. Add 7 children, one at a time until mixture is smooth and is able to handle any emergency with ease and skill. Stir in 1/2 c. sunshine, a dash of tribulation, and 30 years of sitting at ball games. Gradually mix in 2 daughters-in-law, 2 sons-in-law and 14 grandchildren. Bake for 350 episodes of Perry Mason, Matlock or any detective show. Serve with wheat chex and a banana. For best results: Be willing to share this recipe with others as needed.

About the Authors

BONNIE BAILEY

Mix 1 towhead with 2 fantastic parents (no substitutes). Place in a mountain valley and allow to grow in a loving home. Fold in 2 brothers and 4 sisters (stiffly beaten). Gradually add in 2 c. love for God and man, 1 c. chores, 1/2 c. athleticism and a dash of sarcasm (okay, maybe more). Throw in 1 college degree, 1 foreign language, 8 bars of music and an array of unmastered talents. Bake until golden blonde, keeping busy always. For best results: top with 1 suitcase (packed) and send on an occasional adventure.

Check out our other Pie Plate Patterns

10 patterns made with 10" squares

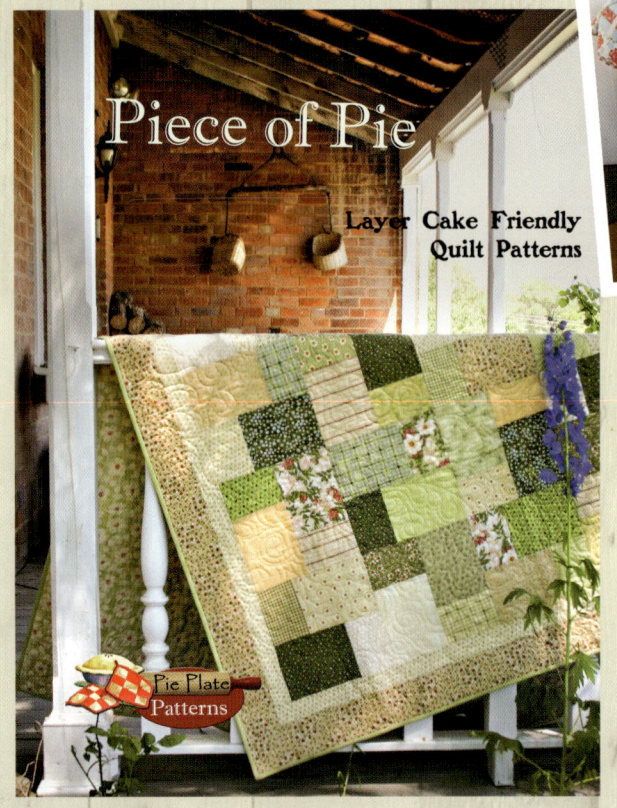

Piece of Pie
Layer Cake Friendly Quilt Patterns

www.pieplatepatterns.com